CH

Cosmetologist

Earning $50,000–$100,000 with a High School Diploma or Less

Earning $50,000–$100,000
with a High School Diploma or Less

Cosmetologist

CHRISTIE MARLOWE

MASON CREST

Mason Crest
450 Parkway Drive, Suite D
Broomall, PA 19008
www.masoncrest.com

Printed in the United States of America.

First printing
9 8 7 6 5 4 3 2 1

Series ISBN: 978-1-4222-2886-9
ISBN: 978-1-4222-2891-3
ebook ISBN: 978-1-4222-8927-3

The Library of Congress has cataloged the
hardcopy format(s) as follows:

Library of Congress Cataloging-in-Publication Data

Marlowe, Christie.
  Cosmetologist / Christie Marlowe.
     pages cm. – (Earning $50,000 - $100,000 with a high school diploma or less)
  Audience: Grade 7 to 8.
  Includes bibliographical references and index.
  ISBN 978-1-4222-2891-3 (hardcover) – ISBN 978-1-4222-2886-9 (series) – ISBN 978-1-4222-8927-3 (ebook)
  1. Beauty culture–Vocational guidance–Juvenile literature. 2. Beauty operators–Juvenile literature. I. Title.
  TT958.M37 2014
  646.7'2023–dc23
                              2013011183

Produced by Vestal Creative Services.
www.vestalcreative.com

Contents

CHAPTER 1
Careers Without College

Cosmetologists have turned making people beautiful into a career. Using makeup, hair gel, scissors, and nail polish, cosmetologists spend their time making people look their best.

Cosmetologists include people who work with hair, skin, makeup, and nails. All cosmetologists work with physical appearance, and use special techniques to make people look more beautiful.

But cosmetology is more than just giving makeovers and cutting hair. Karen Gordon, a cosmetologist who owns her own salon, describes why

Cosmetologists need to enjoy interacting with people. In order to bring out the best in someone's appearance, you need to be able to sense who the person really is by listening carefully to what she says and observing her facial cues.

COSMETOLOGIST

she loves being a cosmetologist: "I always loved hair and fashion, and I love the **service industry**," Karen explains. "There is an old saying that you give what you hope to get back in return. I love making people look and feel better about themselves, and I love it when people make me feel that way too." Karen gets a lot of satisfaction from her job because she feels like she's helping people. People feel good about looking beautiful, and she in turn feels good for helping her customers.

You'll find cosmetologists in **salons** and **spas**. You might even see them on TV or as the authors of books. You'll definitely see their work everywhere—fancy hairstyles, new haircuts, manicures, and makeovers are all the work of cosmetologists.

The women and men who choose cosmetology as a career know a lot. They know exactly how to make anyone look their best. However, only a few cosmetologists learned their job in college. Instead, most of them took a different path.

Looking at the Words

The **service industry** is all the businesses that do work for customers. Cosmetology, banking, health care, and entertainment are all part of the service industry.

Salons are stores where beauty work is done.

Spas are business establishments focused on health, relaxation, and beauty treatment, including massages, steam baths, and exercise.

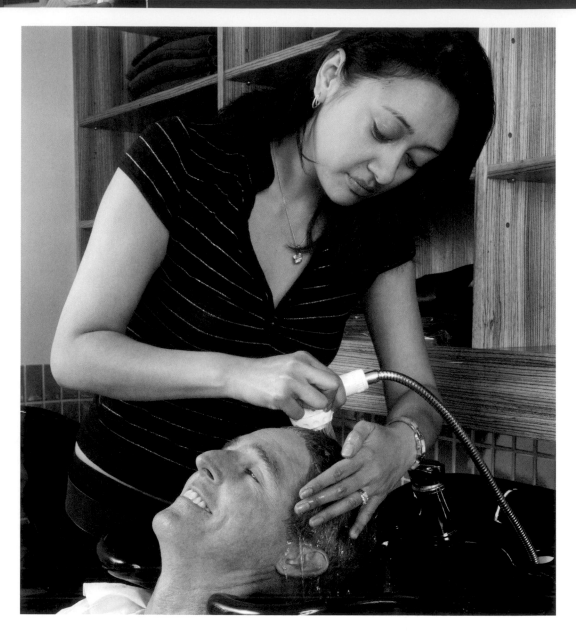

As a cosmetologist, you must be comfortable doing intimate things for people you don't know—things like washing their hair, touching them, holding their fingers and toes. If you're comfortable, your customer will be more likely to be comfortable too.

Deciding on College (or Not)

Deciding whether or not to attend college is a very big decision. Some young people know they want to go to college. Their families probably support their decisions. Their families will probably help them pay for college as well.

Other young people are ready to make money, not spend it on college. Colleges can be very expensive. Many schools cost $40,000, $50,000, or more a year. Although not all colleges are quite that expensive, they may still cost too much for some families to afford.

For other young people, college might not be the best place to learn. Not everyone learns best in a classroom; many people would rather learn by doing, not sitting in a class. And not every job can be learned in college. If you want to be a mechanic, a plumber, or a cosmetologist, you don't need to go to college. You will definitely need to learn plenty of things to be good in these jobs—but you don't have to go to a four-year college to learn them.

You have lots of choices after high school. If a four-year college isn't right for you, maybe a technical school is. Technical schools are also called **trade** schools or **vocational** schools. At a technical school, students learn the skills and knowledge they need for a particular job.

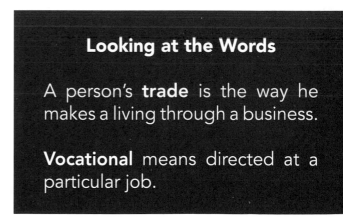

Looking at the Words

A person's **trade** is the way he makes a living through a business.

Vocational means directed at a particular job.

If you take a cosmetology class at a trade school, you will probably practice on mannequins before working with flesh-and-blood people.

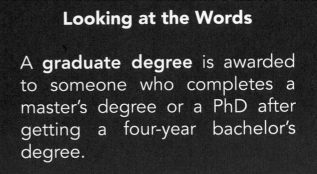

Students study for a year or two before they graduate, and then they can look for a job. Technical schools teach all sorts of jobs, from hair styling to medical assisting to woodworking. Other jobs, however, require a four-year college degree (or even a **graduate degree**). Teachers, engineers, and librarians, for example, have all earned at least a bachelor's degree in their fields.

Apprenticeships are another choice for people who don't want or need to go to college. Like technical schools, apprenticeships teach you how to do a specific job. Apprentices learn how to do the most basic things in their fields by working on the job. A cosmetology apprentice at a hair salon, for example, might learn how to wash customers' hair, clean the salon, and start to cut basic styles. The longer an apprentice works, the more he learns.

No matter what you decide—whether to go to college or take a different route—you'll have to be prepared to work hard. Going straight to a job after high school doesn't mean you have a free pass to be lazy! You'll still have lots to learn, and you will need to show that you are willing to work hard.

An Inspired Job

Many cosmetologists knew they wanted to work with hair and make-up since they were young. Most did not go to college, because they didn't need to. Instead, they learned how to be cosmetologists right

A makeup artist needs to enjoy bringing out the best in others' appearance.

COSMETOLOGIST

away so they could start doing what they loved as soon as possible. Today they can't imagine themselves doing anything else!

In an online article, celebrity makeup artist Carmindy tells the story of why she was **inspired** to keep going with cosmetology. As a teenager,

Carmindy worked at a Marle Norman makeup counter at the mall, giving people makeovers. She says, "One day I was standing at the Merle Norman counter, my brushes at the ready, my favorite lipsticks lined up. A woman with deep creases etched in her forehead came in. 'Do you think you could help me?' she asked hesitantly. 'I'd be glad to,' I said.

"She sank into the chair opposite me. 'I need a complete makeover,' she said. She had a pretty smile, but there was something so sad about her. She could hardly glance in the mirror before turning away, and I wondered what made her feel so unhappy with herself."

Carmindy began to do what she did best. "'Let's start with some foundation,' I said. I went through several to find just the right shade that would bring out her skin's glow. There's something very **intimate** about putting makeup on someone. You're leaning close to her, touching her face. It feels natural to start chatting. And that's what I did with her, as I did with all my clients. I wanted to know something about them— where they lived, what they liked to do, how many children they had. If I saw a spark, I'd get a better idea of what made them tick. But there didn't seem to be anything this woman was passionate about.

"I swirled some blush on, and all at once tears started rolling down her cheeks. 'I'm so sorry,' I said, getting her a tissue. 'Are you okay? Was it something I did?' She shook her head. 'It's my husband,' she

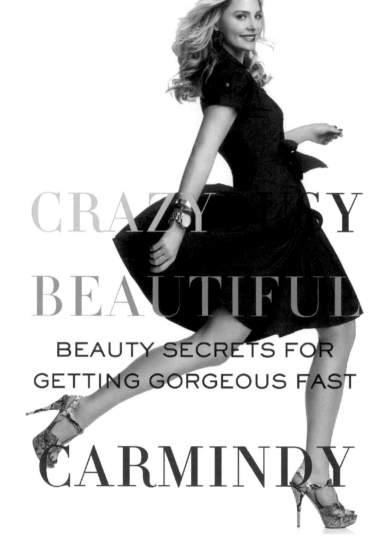

CRAZY BUSY
BEAUTIFUL

BEAUTY SECRETS FOR
GETTING GORGEOUS FAST

CARMINDY

Crazy Busy Beautiful is a collection of beauty tips from Carmindy as well as from everyday women. Some of the secrets are really quirky (for example, one woman uses snail slime to clear up her acne!). It's a fun, positive book, though, that has helped build Carmindy's career.

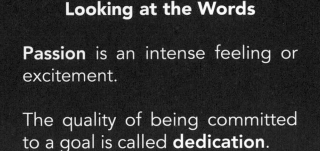

said. 'Nothing I do ever pleases him. He criticizes everything—my cooking, my clothes, my looks.'"

Carmindy continues with her story: "She talked some more and I listened while I worked, applying a sheer eye shadow, dabbing gloss on her lips. I didn't feel qualified to give her advice about mar-

riage—I was just a teenager, after all—but I wanted to show her how lovely she was. Her smile was warm and her eyes, even when she was so upset, were soft and kind.

"For a while we were both silent, that silence of two people concentrating together. I did my best to make my work convey to her what my mother said to me, 'You're beautiful just as you are.' When I was finished, I turned her chair to face the mirror. And in that moment, she saw it. 'You've made me beautiful!' she exclaimed. 'No,' said, 'I didn't do that. That's how you were made.'"

Carmindy says that day, and others like them, convinced her she needed to be a cosmetologist. She wasn't sure where her path would lead next, but she knew she had to try. She loved helping women see how beautiful they were, and cosmetology was the right career.

Because of her **passion** and her **dedication**, Carmindy has become a successful makeup artist. She has worked with celebrities, she stars on TLC's *What Not to Wear,* and she has written several books. She is happy with her life as a cosmetologist, just like she knew she would be as a teenager at the mall.

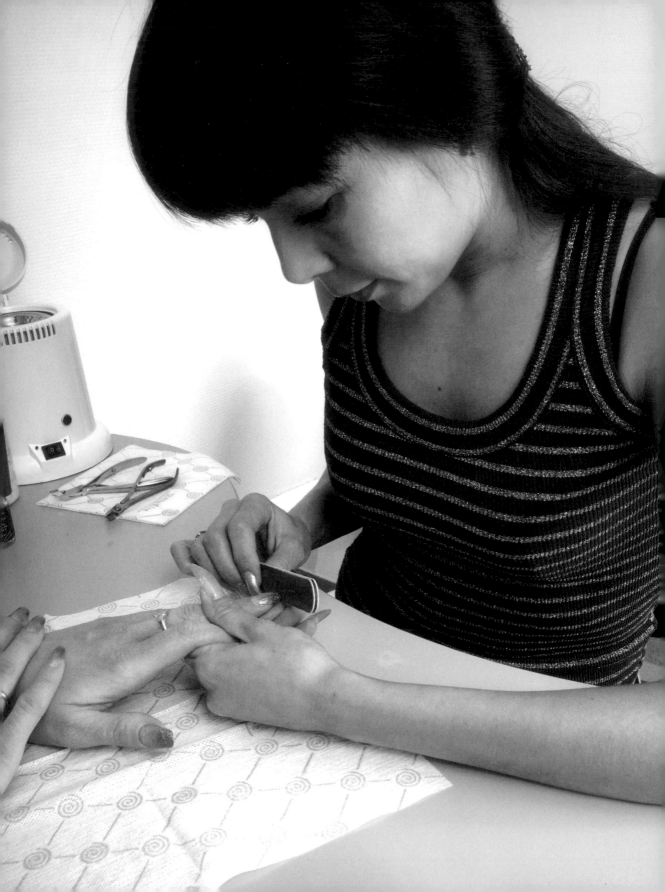

CHAPTER 2

What Do Cosmotologists Do?

n 2010, there were 627,700 cosmetologists in the United States. Some cut and style hair. Others work with makeup. Still others give manicures and pedicures. Finally, a few cosmetologists focus on skincare and skin treatments. All those hundreds of thousands of cosmetologists keep people looking beautiful.

If you're looking into cosmetology as a career, you have a lot of choices. You can explore different areas of beauty and decide which one is the best for you.

More and more men are choosing careers in cosmetology.

Are Men Cosmetologists?

Plenty of men are cosmetologists! About 90 percent of cosmetologists are women. In other words, nine out of ten cosmetologists are women. But that means 10 percent of those 627,700 cosmetologists are men—over 62,000 of them to be exact. And more and more men are starting out in the field. Cosmetology schools report that numbers of male students are rising. There are even famous male cosmetologists with their own lines of beauty products, like Vidal Sassoon and John Frieda.

Hairdressers

Hairdressers are the people who cut and style hair. Most people go to the hair dresser every few months or so. Hairdressers can change your style with a few snips or maybe some hair dye.

Hairdressers have to understand hair. They can't just take scissors and chop away at a customer's hair. Instead, they study the customer and figure out exactly what she wants and what would look best. Then the hairdresser must do her best to make it happen.

Customers want a variety of things done to their hair. They want it trimmed or cut. They want it died, straightened, or curled. They want it washed and blow dried perfectly. They might want **extensions**. A hairdresser needs to know how to do all those things.

Besides fashion and styling, hairdressers know about the structure and health of hair. They can give customers advice on making hair healthier, they know what products to use, and they avoid damaging hair in the salon.

Some hairdressers specialize in certain kinds of customers. Barbers often cut men's hair. Other hairdressers work with women's hair, curly hair, or African American hair. Each sort of hairdresser has to know how to give customers what they need.

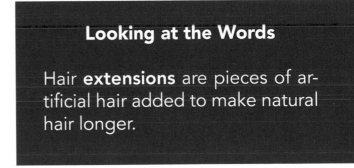

Looking at the Words

Hair **extensions** are pieces of artificial hair added to make natural hair longer.

Karen Gordon focuses on cutting and styling hair. In an interview, she discusses her everyday duties. "Along with all of the day-to-day management responsibilities of running a successful salon," says Karen, "my responsibilities as a hairdresser are: Provide a thorough

Some makeup artists work with professional photographers.

and professional **consultation** with my clients, perform to the best of my abilities the services that we agree upon, and recommend proper techniques and products so that my clients can maintain their style/color at home."

She goes on to say, "It is also my responsibility to pro-

vide a clean and safe environment for my clients and co-workers, and to receive continuing education about the latest trends and **technologies** for my industry. I usually see a client every forty-five minutes, or every hour if they require more complicated services. I don't take a lunch break, and I prefer to eat when I am between clients. That's pretty normal for a hairdresser!"

Karen is happy working with her customers. She explains, "I suppose that it would be fun to be a hairdresser backstage at fashion shows and hang out with models and celebrities. But, if I had really wanted to do that, I would have gone out and done that years ago." Her busy schedule keeps her working hard, but it's work she finds worthwhile.

Makeup Artists

Other cosmetologists work mostly with makeup. Lots of makeup artists work with ordinary people who want to add some glamour to their lives. They give women makeovers and apply makeup for special events like weddings. These makeup artists can listen to customers and figure out what they want. They also know which colors of makeup work best

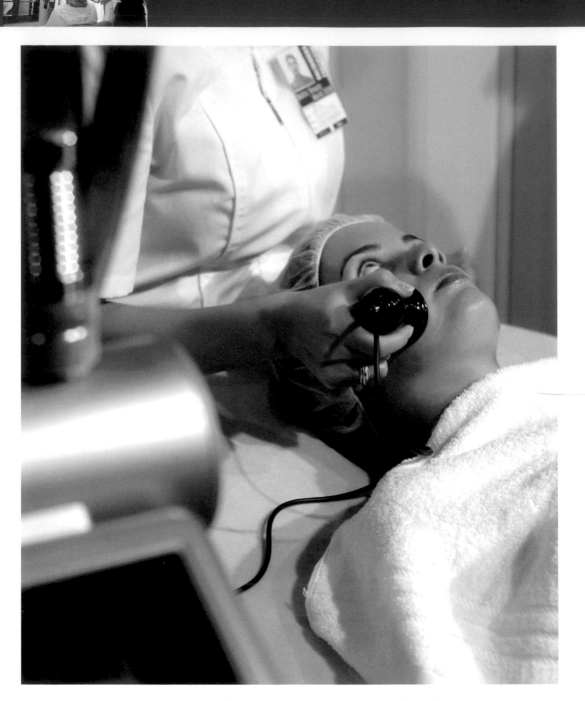

Estheticians use high-tech equipment to care for their customer's skin.

with different skin tones, and how to work with all kinds of makeup, like eyeliner, foundation, and mascara.

Other makeup artists work with celebrities and other actors. Film studios use makeup artists to give actors the right look for their roles. Special-effects makeup artists know how to turn actors into animals, monsters, or older or younger versions of themselves using makeup techniques. TV studios will also hire makeup artists to work with newscasters and talk show hosts.

Skincare Specialists

Cosmetologists who deal with skin care work in esthetics. Estheticians, as they're known, help customers take care of their skin.

Estheticians are trained in several different skin-care techniques. They can give customers facials, **exfoliate** their skin, or remove unwanted hair.

Although most estheticians aren't medical professionals, they sometimes work with doctors. If an esthetician sees something wrong with a customer's skin, he can recommend the customer go see a doctor. Estheticians should be able to spot things that might need a doctor's attention.

Some professionals are actually medical estheticians. They have had more training in medical knowledge about skin. Medical estheticians can work in places like **dermatology** offices or plastic surgery offices.

Looking at the Words

To **exfoliate** means to rub the body to remove dead skin cells.

Dermatology is the study and treatment of skin disorders.

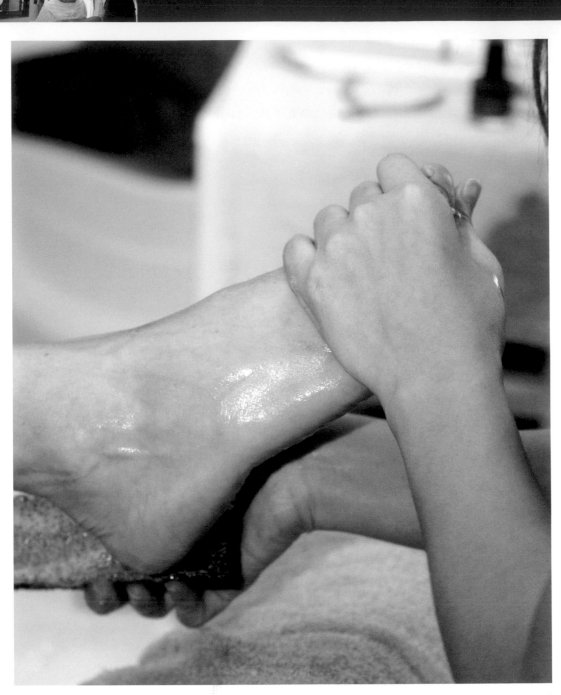

Some manicurists will include hand or foot massages as part of their services.

Manicurists

Manicurists focus on nails. They clean, trim, and polish finger- and toe-nails. They also know how to work with fake nails. Some manicurists are artists, creating pictures, designs, and patterns on the tiny surfaces of nails. Many also know how to massage hands and feet, and make the skin on hands and feet healthier and beautiful.

Manicurists might work in a salon where other beauty treatments are available, or they might work in nail salons entirely dedicated to manicures and pedicures.

Daily Life

The good thing about cosmetology is that you have a lot of room to decide what you want your schedule to look like. Some cosmetologists work part time. They have another job or they take care of their children at home. They might work twenty hours a week, or a little more or a little fewer.

Other cosmetologists own their own businesses. Karen, for example, owns her own salon with her husband, and has hired more than twenty other people to work for her. Owning your own business is a lot of work. Salon owners might work more than forty hours a week. They work in the evenings and sometimes six or seven days a week, depending on how many customers they want to have.

Cosmetologists work at a variety of places. Many work in a salon or spa with other cosmetologists. There may be anywhere from two to dozens of cosmetologists all working in the same space. Other cosmetologists work at home or in businesses they own themselves.

A beauty salon could be as fancy as this one—or it could be just a room in a cosmetologist's home.

Customers come to their homes to get their hair cut or makeup done. Sometimes hairdressers or makeup artists will even travel around to their customers. These cosmetologists can make their own schedules, since they work for themselves. Smaller numbers of cosmetologists work at hotels, resorts, and spas.

Looking at the Words

Someone who behaves **professionally** treats his job seriously, according to practices and rules that are accepted for that job.

All cosmetologists do have some things in common. Salons and spas are businesses and have to be run **professionally**. Cosmetologists keep their workspaces clean, including their tools. Unclean combs, scissors, and makeup brushes can spread diseases, so cosmetologists have to be extra careful. Many cosmetologists also have to schedule appointments, keep track of customer records, and use cash registers for payments. Helping run the business is part of being a cosmetologist.

Even More Careers

Becoming a cosmetologist opens up a whole world of possibilities! Besides working in a salon, you could be a beauty magazine editor, work for a makeup company, manage a spa, teach at a cosmetology school, become a fashion show stylist, or start your own beauty care product company. Cosmetology can take you lots of places!

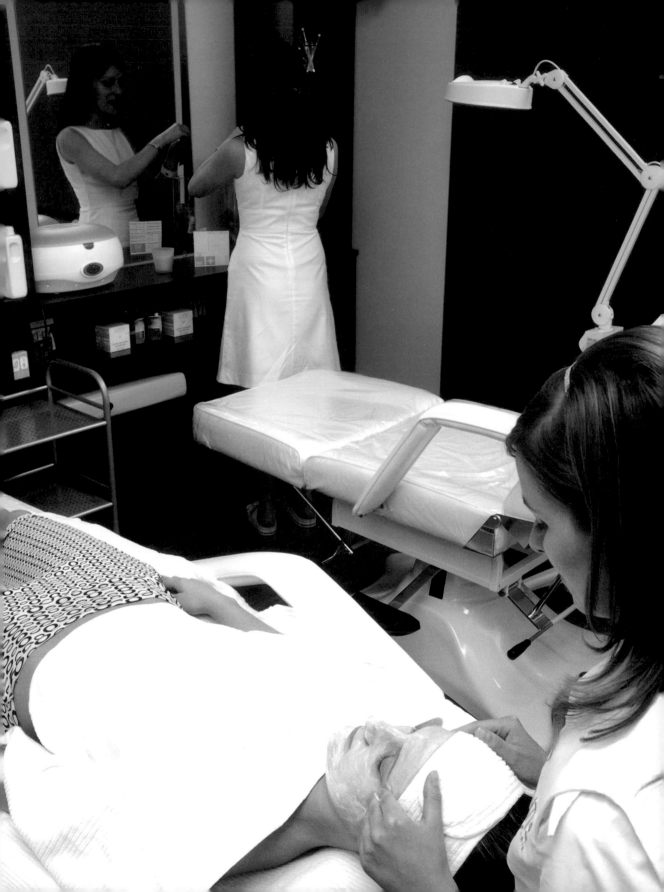

CHAPTER 3

How Can I Become a Cosmetologist?

You won't need to go to college to train to be a cosmetologist. However, you'll still need to learn a lot before you can start cutting hair, painting nails, or giving makeovers.

Carmindy describes her rise to the top of the cosmetologist world: "When I was fifteen years old I became obsessed with makeup and began practicing on myself and friends. I would tear out pictures from magazines, read every book out there about fashion

Carmindy has always believed in herself. According to her website, when she looks in the mirror each morning, she tells herself, "Today I am going to rock this world."

COSMETOLOGIST

and dream big, picturing myself traveling the world over, painting faces. One day I discovered that my friend's father was a makeup artist for a TV show in Hollywood. I would go over to his house and question him for hours about the **industry**, checking out his makeup and toolbox and learning about how to break into the biz. There was no real industry

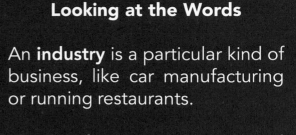

then and I had to do a lot of digging to find out how to become a makeup artist." Carmindy started with passion, and then figured out whether she could make that passion into a career.

As it turned out, she definitely *could* make a career out of makeup. She got some more early experience. "I kept practicing doing makeup on friends," she says, "and when I was seventeen I got a job working at a cosmetic counter at the mall. I then signed up at a hair and makeup agency as an apprentice and for two years worked on set assisting. I cleaned brushes, fetched coffee, organized lipsticks and watched, listened and learned." At seventeen, she also started taking makeup classes. "I took a few courses in LA from a makeup artist named Maurice Stein. He owned a makeup company and school called Cinema Secrets. This was a man I wanted to impress with my talent because he was so **seasoned** and a great teacher. When he always seemed to give me the highest score in the class I knew I was on the right path."

Then Carmindy got a big opportunity. She had earned a reputation as a hard worker on fashion sets. She says, "The photographer's assistants would ask me if I wanted to do test shooting over the weekend with new

Lots of teenagers experiment with cutting each other's hair. If this is something you love to do, you might consider making a career out of it.

models and I would do it for free to build my **portfolio**. One magic day the professional makeup artist I was assisting became ill and I had to step in and do a swimwear catalog and the photographer liked my work better and that was the beginning of my career."

From there, Carmindy took every opportunity she could. Eventually she started traveling to do fashion shoots around the country. And then the makers of the TV show *What Not to Wear* noticed her. She became the makeover artist on the show, started her own line of beauty products, and began writing books. Now she is one of the most famous makeup artists around.

Not everyone's path will be exactly like Carmindy's. Most cosmetologists don't become famous as TV stars. But they do share some

things with Carmindy—the willingness to work hard and a love of the job.

Early Experience

Many future cosmetologists realize they want to work with hair, make-up, nails, and skin early on. They discover they like to cut their own hair, or they give friends beauty advice. Like Carmindy, some young people start experimenting on themselves and friends.

Sometimes high schools offer vocational classes, where students can explore future careers. If you think you might be interested in cosmetology, you can ask around to see if your school has one of these programs. Then you can take a class or two in cosmetology and see what you think. If you don't like your classes, then you know cosmetology might not be for you. If you do like them, you'll know you want to keep learning cosmetology and maybe make a career out of it.

Even if your school doesn't have cosmetology program, you'll still need to finish high school. Many cosmetology positions require you to have a high school diploma. For people who don't finish high school as a teenager, a **GED** is usually okay, instead of a high school diploma.

Looking at the Words

An artist's **portfolio** is a collection of his work organized for other people to see.

GED stands for General Educational Development. If a person does not get a high school degree, she can later study high school subjects and take the GED tests. Passing the GED tests is equivalent to getting a high school diploma.

Be Prepared

Successful cosmetologists love their jobs, but not everything about their work is perfect. It's a good idea to get to know some of the downsides of cosmetology so you'll be prepared. For example, cosmetologists often stand for eight, nine, ten or more hours every day. They get tired feet, shoulders, and backs. They need to take time to relax and move around. The long hours and work on evenings and weekends also tire people out. Cosmetologists sometimes also get fed up with how much their jobs focus on physical appearance. However, cosmetologists who really love their profession focus on the great parts of the job, so they can deal with a bad day now and then.

Cosmetology School

Cosmetology school is one of the best places to learn how to be a hairdresser, barber, or makeup artist. At the end, you'll get a degree or a certificate that lets you start working as a cosmetologist.

Some cosmetology programs are more general, and students learn about each type of cosmetology. Others let students pick one kind of cosmetology to study and get really good at that one thing.

Students may take courses in hair cutting and styling, hair coloring, manicures and pedicures, facials, makeup, and more. Some students, like those studying esthetics, also take science courses like chemistry

and **anatomy**. Other classes might include salon management and finances.

You'll get experience actually doing hair, makeup, and nails while you're at cosmetology school. Many programs have a salon where customers can come in for a low price, or even for free. Customers get haircuts, makeup, and manicures done by cosmetology students. School salons are a good way for students to practice with real-life clients before they start a job.

Cosmetology programs cost less than college, but they can still be expensive depending on where you go. In 2012, the average cost of cosmetology school was between $10,000 and $20,000. Specific programs focused on makeup artistry or esthetics are often less expensive, though. They can be between $3,000 and $5,000. You'll also need to buy your own books and supplies, like scissors, makeup, and aprons.

You might be able to get financial aid like **student loans** or **scholarships**. Schools know that not everyone can afford $20,000, so they give money to many students.

Cosmetology school takes anywhere from nine months to a couple of years to finish. However, shorter programs don't always give you enough training. You want to find a program that gives you enough support to really learn new skills. You don't want to graduate and realize you can't get a job anywhere because you don't know enough!

Many cosmetology schools will require that you buy a head like this one, which you will use for practicing your lessons.

Look around for a cosmetology school that is right for you. If you want to focus on nail care, make sure the schools you're applying to have nail care. If you can't afford an expensive school, look around for cheaper schools that will still give you the skills you need. Go visit the school and talk to the students and teachers. Are students happy there? Do the students who graduate get good jobs right away? Ask questions so you know what you're getting yourself into.

Apprenticeships

Cosmetologists have the choice of doing apprenticeships before they get full jobs. Apprenticeships offer on-the-job training. They also can take longer than going to cosmetology school. Some people get most of their training through an apprenticeship, and not a cosmetology school. Check your state to see if you're allowed to do that. You may also be able to get an apprenticeship after cosmetology school.

That's what Karen did. She first went to cosmetology school to learn the basics. Then she got an apprenticeship at a salon, so she could learn even more.

"I did shampooing, sweeping the floors, etc.," she explains. "It was hard work, but I learned a lot. After I graduated from cosmetology school, I worked as an apprentice for a year so that I could improve my skills."

Karen suggests that new cosmetologists should do what she did. "When you get out of cosmetology school, become an apprentice in a great salon," Karen advises. "Cosmetology school teaches you the basics. Take another year and invest in your career. Love what you do, and the money will come." After she finished her apprenticeship, she went on to co-own her own salon. Cosmetology school and the apprenticeship paid off!

What Will I Actually Learn?

According to the Trade Schools, Colleges, and Universities website, a lot of cosmetology schools teach the topics covered by one textbook in particular, called *Milady's Standard Cosmetology*. Among the topics students learn are:

- basic life skills (such as setting goals and maintaining a positive attitude)
- developing a professional image
- communication skills
- infection control (including how to prevent the spread of hepatitis, HIV, or other infectious viruses or bacteria in a salon)
- general anatomy and physiology
- basics of chemistry and electricity
- hair and scalp characteristics
- principles of hair design (such as how to enhance a person's look based on facial shape)
- basic hair care (shampooing, rinsing, and conditioning)
- basic haircutting (including core cuts)
- hairstyling (including how to use the proper tools and techniques)
- hair braiding and braid extensions
- hair coloring
- chemical hair texturing
- wigs and other hair enhancements
- properties of skin and nails (including how they grow)

- skin diseases and disorders
- hair removal (such as waxing and tweezing)
- performing basic facials
- makeup
- nail diseases and disorders
- performing manicures
- performing pedicures
- creating a résumé and portfolio
- preparing for job interviews
- basic business skills
- preparing for state licensure exams

Licensing

Even after all that, cosmetologists need to take one more step before they can work—they need to get licensed. A license is a piece of paper from the government that says a person can legally practice cosmetology. The government doesn't want people working who don't know what they're doing, because cosmetology often involves health issues. For example, if a manicurist doesn't really know how to cut cuticles right, she may cause a customer's nails to get infected.

To get a license, you usually have to have a high school diploma (or a GED), be at least sixteen, and have graduated from a cosmetology school. Every state has different licensing rules, so check with your state before you make any decisions about how to learn cosmetology. Some states let you get a license after you finish an apprenticeship rather than cosmetology school.

You also need to take a test to get your license. The test has a written part and sometimes a second part where you will need to show your actual skills. You'll see questions about sanitation, safety, chemicals used in cosmetology, skin care, salon management, and more. If you have worked hard at learning what you need to know, you'll know exactly what you need in order to pass the test.

Once you pass your exam, you'll need to get your license renewed every few years. If you move to another state, you might need to get a new license too. Most states don't accept licenses from other states.

What Else Do I Need?

Learning cosmetology skills is only half of what you need in order to become a successful cosmetologist. You also need certain **qualities**.

The U.S. Bureau of Labor Statistics lists some qualities it is important for cosmetologists to have. Cosmetologists must be creative, for example. Customers will come in and ask for a certain hairstyle or makeup. A cosmetologist has to know how to make that happen by picturing it in her head and then doing it. Or the customer might tell a cosmetologist she wants something new, and to do whatever he wants. The cosmetologist has to be able to think of a new style and create it on the spot. In a way, cosmetologists are artists, who sculpt or paint the human body.

Cosmetologists have to have good customer-service skills too. They work with customers almost all day. Cosmetologists tend to be friendly, and open to meeting and talking to new people. Even if they're in a bad mood, they leave it behind them while they work. Cosmetologists always have to be friendly to customers.

Often, cosmetologists love their jobs because they get to talk to so many people. "You have to love serving people, and you have to be patient," says Karen. "It takes time and perseverance to become a

great hairdresser and to build a **clientele**, but the rewards are so worth it." She goes on to say, "'My clients are the most wonderful people. I have learned so much from them about all sorts of things over the years. They have truly enriched my life."

Time-management skills are another important quality cosmetologists need. This is the ability to balance a busy schedule. Cosmetologists might see ten customers a day. They always have new and returning customers calling to make appointments. They can't book two appointments at once. Cosmetologists also often have cleaning and **bookkeeping** to do, so they have to leave themselves breaks in customers. A cosmetologist with good time-management skills will be able to do all that without a problem.

Karen adds a quality to this list: patience. "A lot of people get frustrated one or two years into the profession because they feel things are not happening 'fast enough for them,'" Karen explains. "It takes time to become really good at hairdressing, and it takes time to build a clientele. Too many people drop out just as they are getting along."

Cosmetologists need the patience to get better at their trade slowly and to constantly learn new things. A new cosmetologist might also find that it takes a few years to get loyal customers. If they are patient, they'll find customers who will come back again and again. Once that happens, they will truly be successful at their jobs!

CHAPTER 4

How Much
Can I Make?

Hard-working cosmetologists can expect to make a good living. They may not be rich or famous, but they'll be earning money for doing what they love.

The Average

The U.S. Bureau of Labor Statistics says cosmetologists made an average of $10.94

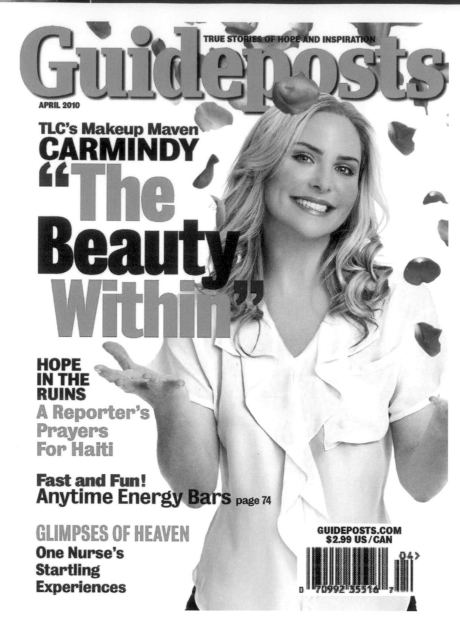

TRUE STORIES OF HOPE AND INSPIRATION

Guideposts

APRIL 2010

TLC's Makeup Maven
CARMINDY
"The Beauty Within"

**HOPE
IN THE
RUINS**
A Reporter's
Prayers
For Haiti

**Fast and Fun!
Anytime Energy Bars** page 74

GLIMPSES OF HEAVEN
One Nurse's
Startling
Experiences

GUIDEPOSTS.COM
$2.99 US/CAN

04>
D 70992 35516 7

As a celebrity cosmologist, Carmindy appears in magazines and on TV. She makes lots of money, but she still believes that the most important thing is the beauty that's inside people, no matter what they look like on the outside.

46 COSMETOLOGIST

an hour in 2010. Cosmetologists usually work by the hour. As a yearly income, that works out to be a little over $22,000, working forty hours a week all year long.

In reality, cosmetologists make all different amounts of money. A cosmetologist just starting out might make a little less than $10.94 an hour. They

don't have much practice yet, and they won't have built up enough customers who come back again and again. The longer they stick with their jobs, though, the more money they'll make. Cosmetologists who choose to work part time may also make less per year, because they are only working ten, twenty, or thirty hours a week. A cosmetologist who works twenty hours a week for $10.94 an hour will make about $11,000 over a whole year.

Older cosmetologists who have been working for a while might make a lot more than $10.94 an hour. They are very skilled and have a lot of customers. They have customers who know them and love their work. They may own their own salons, like Karen, and make a lot more money.

Cosmetologists make different amounts of money depending on where they work too. A makeup artist who works in a big city will likely make a lot more money than a makeup artist who works in a tiny town. Of course, it will also be more expensive to live in the big city, and the cosmetologist will have to spend more money on housing, food, and other things.

The Bureau of Labor Statistics average also doesn't include tips. For each haircut, manicure, or makeover, a cosmetologist usually gets a tip from the customer. How much the tip is depends on where the cosmetologist works. A hairdresser at a **chain** salon might make a couple of

How Much Can I Make?

dollars as a tip, but hairdressers at fancier salons may make $10 or more. Successful cosmetologists might also get bonuses from the salons where they work. Salons give out bonuses for bringing in a lot of new customers or selling a lot of beauty products.

The top 10 percent of cosmetologists make $41,500 or more. At the higher end, the most experienced cosmetologists can make $50,000 a year, including tips and bonuses.

Benefits

Benefits are extra things you get from an employer, like health care and vacation days. Some salons offer benefits, but a lot don't. Look around for a job that gives you health insurance, paid vacation days, and overtime pay. Benefits can be hard to find, though, so you might need to be willing to work for a few years without them, until you have more experience.

Star Cosmetologists

Some young cosmetologists dream about becoming rich and famous. If you're one of them, you'll need to work hard, meet new people, and have a little luck. But anything is possible!

Celebrity cosmetologists have some things in common. They are really good at what they do, for one. They have practiced for years,

A Few Famous Cosmetologists

You may have heard of some of these famous cosmetologists, who enjoy fame, money, and a great job they love.

- Madam C.J. Walker (Sarah Breedlove) was the first African American to make hair care products, and the first African American women to become a millionaire. She was born in 1867. She created a line of hair care products for scalp health. She taught other black women how to take care of their hair, and worked for black rights.
- John Frieda is a British celebrity hairstylist. He started a line of hair products that are sold all over the world.
- Sally Hershberger is a hairstylist who is well known for creating Meg Ryan's famous haircut in the 1990s. She has also appeared on TV shows like *Shear Genius* and *America's Next Top Model*. Her haircuts are expensive—she used to charge $600 a haircut, and they're even more expensive today!
- Paul Mitchell is a Scottish hairstylist. He ran several famous salons and eventually started his own line of products. Mitchell's son is also a famous cosmetologist.
- Vidal Sassoon is a British hairdresser who made a big name for himself starting in the 1960s. He first created a famous short haircut, and then went on to start a line of hair-care products still sold today.

and they have perfected their techniques. They're also really passionate about their work. They love what they do, and they do it all the time. They knew they had to meet the right people and convince them they were amazing cosmetologists, so they also have a lot of confidence in themselves.

Some cosmetologists work with movie or TV stars. You can find their hair and makeup work on screens around the world. Others work on fashion shoots, for magazines or advertisements. A few even work for fashion shows, doing the hair and makeup for models. Cosmetologists like this make more money than the average cosmetologist.

Some cosmetologists make money a different way. They start their own beauty product lines, which bring in extra money. Or they write a book about beauty advice, which also makes money. Cosmetologists may also be on TV shows. All these kinds of cosmetologists become stars themselves!

Money and More

The best jobs earn a good living, but they are also fun and help you learn new things and feel **fulfilled**. Cosmetologists love their jobs because of the people they meet, and because they love being creative with nail polish, makeup, scissors, and more.

Take Carmindy. She's on the TV show *What Not to Wear*, has her own line of beauty products, writes books, and gives interviews. You might think her favorite part of her job is the fame and fortune. However, Carmindy says otherwise. Even at a young age, Carmindy loved doing makeovers, and she wasn't very interested in the money she could get by doing them. As a teenager selling makeup at a Merle Norman counter at the mall, she had to sell makeup as part of her job. However, she says,

"You know how I said I was more interested in the women themselves than in selling them Merle Norman products? Well, I got fired for not selling enough." She didn't care enough about the extra money she would get if she sold makeup—she just wanted to work with people and make them beautiful.

She goes on to say, "I promptly got a job doing makeovers at another place in the mall. I moved on from there, working with women all over the world (some models, some not), and eventually established myself as a top makeup artist. Today, I'm the makeup artist for TLC's hit TV show *What Not to Wear*. I write books on beauty (the latest is *Crazy Busy Beautiful*). I've co-created a line of cosmetics." Her love of makeup and working with women of all types led to her fame and her money. The fame and money are great, but they wouldn't be worth it if Carmindy didn't love her job.

Carmindy explains some of the **perks** of her job today: "Being a makeup artist is wonderful. There is no better job in the world then making women feel and look incredible. Our entire society has us feeling insecure about ourselves and if you can make just one women feel gorgeous and happy it is all worth it. Not to mention the new and interesting people you get to meet, the exotic traveling you get to do and also the escape from a regular 9-to-5 which is just not for me."

Carmindy and thousands of other cosmetologists—rich or not—are doing what they love to do. You can't have a better life than that!

Looking at the Words

Someone who is **fulfilled** is completely content with what she is doing.

Perks are benefits or advantages to having a particular job.

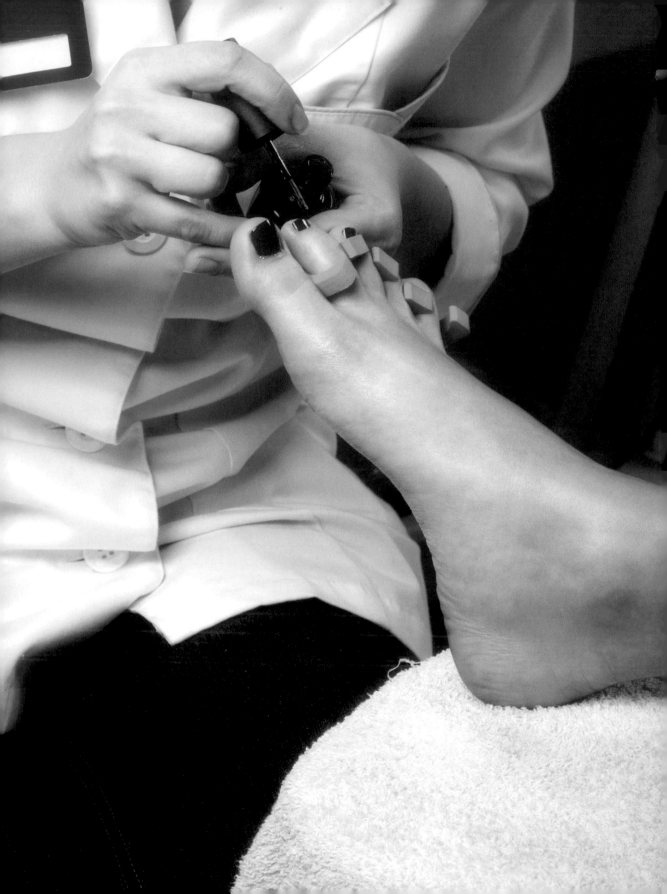

CHAPTER 5

Looking to the Future

The future looks bright for cosmetologists and for young people who are interested in becoming cosmetologists. Cosmetology is a great job option for young people.

If you're thinking about going into cosmetology, you can start practicing and doing some research. Play with makeup, hair, and skin. Practice on friends, family, and yourself. Try out different things and see what you like best. Read about how to apply makeup, do nails, and cut hair.

You can talk to people too. Talk to your guidance counselor at school about becoming a cosmetologist. Your guidance counselor can give you information about different jobs and how to get them. She can point out books and websites you can look at for even more information. Talk to real cosmetologists too—they're the best sources of information. When you get your hair cut, for example, ask the hairdresser lots of questions and find out how she got her job. The more people you talk to, the better you'll understand what cosmetology is like.

The Future of Cosmetology

The U.S. Bureau of Labor Statistics reports jobs for cosmetologists will grow about 16 percent by 2020. Thousands more cosmetologists will be hired over the next few years. People want to be beautiful, so they get facials, have their nails painted, and get their hair cut. They turn to cosmetologists to do all those things.

Job growth is good news Recently, the **economy** has not been very healthy. People have lost their jobs and have had trouble finding new ones, or even finding a first job after high school or college. Luckily, cosmetologists aren't having as much trouble as some other people.

Looking at the Words

The **economy** is the wealth produced by goods and services.

When you **network** with people, you make connections with them by talking about shared experiences and interests. Networking leads to new work opportunities.

Over the next few years, plenty of cosmetologists will retire. Or they will get different jobs or start working part time instead of full time. When all these workers leave, new cosmetologists will have the chance to start their careers. Salons might even expand, as more customers come to them. Those salons will hire new cosmetologists to work with all the new customers.

Cosmetologists will find that getting a job at a fancy salon where the pay is better won't be as easy. High-end salons only take the best cosmetologists who have the most experience. If your goal is to work in one of these salons, it's a good idea to get as much work experience as you can before you start applying. Only the people who work the hardest and **network** with the right people will end up with these jobs.

A cosmetologist at a spa is exfoliating a customer's feet and legs. High-end spas like this one pay their employees well.

Looking to the Future   **55**

Your First Job

Your first job might not be the most glamorous or the best paying. Once you get your license, you'll have to decide what to do next. You'll have to be patient and **persistent**. Finding a job might take a few weeks or even a few months. Apply to lots of places, and keep an open mind. Be confident when you interview. You might even have to prove you know what you're doing in an interview by actually showing your skills on a customer or on a friend you bring with you.

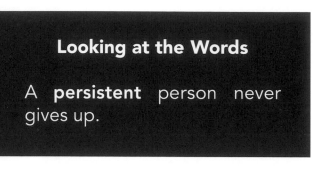

Looking at the Words

A **persistent** person never gives up.

Your first job might turn out to be that you work as an assistant or an apprentice. Be positive, and you'll learn a lot. Work hard. Instead of grumbling while you clean floors and do laundry, watch what your coworkers are doing. Be respectful and offer to help when needed. Once your boss knows you are friendly and a hard worker, you might have opportunities to move up.

When you start working with clients, try your hardest. Be friendly, listen to what your client wants, and do your best work. If your client is happy, he or she will come back again and again to see you. Try to stick with one job for a while. Even if you don't think it's perfect, keep the job for a while. You might end up liking it a lot more. And staying with one job helps you build up clients who know you and want you to cut their hair or do their makeup. When you're ready to move to a different job, some of your clients will come with you.

Don't get frustrated that you don't know everything right away. Cosmetologists work for years to build up their skills. You just have to be

patient—and one day, you'll be styling hair, painting nails, or applying lipstick with the best of them.

Your Future

After you spend some time at your first job, you'll have learned all sorts of new skills and met lots of new people. What's next?

You have a few choices. You could look for a job working in a fancier salon that charges more and is known for good work—and probably pays better too. You could start your own business out of your home, or start your own salon. Owning your own business means you have more control over your job and you will make more money. You could also work as a teacher at a beauty school, start looking for work as a celebrity cosmetologist, or start your own line of beauty products.

Desairology

Desairology is not for everyone, but it can be an adventure for the right person. A desairologist works with dead people, to make them look peaceful and beautiful for funerals. They help make funerals and death a little easier for loved ones. Most desairologists don't work full time. They may also work with living people, or have another job entirely the rest of the time.

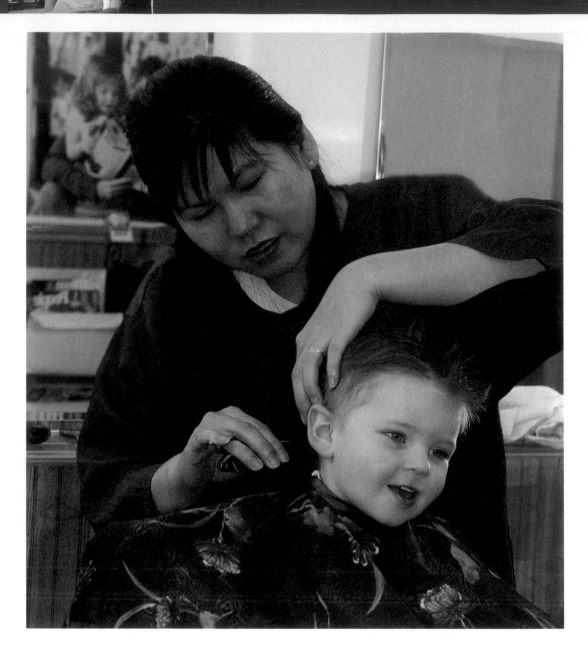

Do you enjoy working with children? Being able to make children relax and feel comfortable while they get their hair cut is a great skill for a cosmetologist to have.

Learn from Carmindy

On her website, Carmindy writes:

"My beauty philosophy is that true beauty is about owning your own individual uniqueness and celebrating who you are. Makeup should be used to enhance your natural beauty never to change it. By using the right products in the right places and sharing my inspirational and positive beauty insight I can help you showcase your best features creating a glow from within and retraining your brain to become the empowered woman you deserve to be! IBy transforming your perception of beauty you can begin to really see it not only in yourself, but also in those around you. You need to accept and love yourself as you are first, then makeup can be a fun and fabulous way to play up your face bringing out your true confidence that is magnetic, contagious and limitless."

If Carmindy's words inspire you, you might just have what it takes to have a successful career in cosmetology!

If you think cosmetology might be for you, start learning now! As Karen, the salon owner says, "I love my work and I love my clients. Surveys show that hairdressers are among the most professionally satisfied people."

What more could you ask?

Find Out More

In Books

Ferguson Publishing. *Cosmetology (Careers in Focus)*. New York: Ferguson Publishing, 2002.

Milady. *Milady's Standard Cosmetology*. Clifton Park, N.Y.: Milady, 2008.

Svitil, Torene and Amy Dunkleburger. *So You Want to Work in Set Design, Costuming, or Make-Up?* Berkeley Heights, N.J.: Enslow Publishers, 2008.

On the Internet

Beauty Schools Directory
www.beautyschoolsdirectory.com/faq/cosmetologist.php

Education-Portal.
Education-portal.com/articles/Cosmetology_Summary_of_
Educational_ Requirements_to_Become_a_Cosmetologist.html

U.S. Bureau of Labor Statistics
www.bls.gov/ooh/personal-care-and-service/barbers-hairdressers-and-
cosmetologists.htm#tab-2

Bibliography

Beauty Schools Directory. "Cosmetologist Job Description and Information." www.beautyschoolsdirectory.com/faq/cosmetologist.php (accessed March 4, 2013).

Curves and Style. "The Inside Scoop with Carmindy." curvesnstyle.com/inside-scoop-with-carmindy1 (accessed March 4, 2013).

Guideposts. "Carmindy's Inspiring Life." www.guideposts.org/inspirational-stories/inspiring-story-about-carmindy-turning-her-life-around (accessed March 4, 2013).

My Footpath. "Cosmetologist Interview." myfootpath.com/career-advice-and-answers/career-interviews/cosmetologist-beautician-career-interview (accessed March 4, 2013).

O Net Online. "Summary Report for: Hairdressers, Hairstylists, and Cosmetologists." www.onetonline.org/link/summary/39-5012.00 (accessed March 4, 2013).

Online Beauty School. "Top 10 Wealthiest Celebrity Cosmetologists." onlinebeautyschool.org/2012/top-10-wealthiest-celebrity-cosmetologists (accessed March 4, 2013).

Trade Schools, Colleges, and Universities. "Cosmetologist Career Information." www.trade-schools.net/career-counselor/cosmetologist-information.asp (accessed March 4, 2013).

U.S. Bureau of Labor Statistics. "Barbers, Hairdressers, and Cosmetologists." www.bls.gov/ooh/personal-care-and-service/barbers-hairdressers-and-cosmetologists.htm#tab-1 (accessed March 4, 2013).

Wisegeek.com. "What Is a Cosmetologist?" www.wisegeek.com/what-is-a-cosmetologist.htm (accessed March 4, 2013).

Index

About the Author

Christie Marlowe was raised in Binghamton, New York, where she lives and works as a writer and web designer. She has a degree in literature, cares strongly about the environment, and spends three or more nights a week wailing on her Telecaster.

Picture Credits

p. 16: William Morrow; p. 32: Carmindy.com; p. 38: Aliex Press;p. 46: Guideposts

Dreamstime Stock Photos
p. 6: Yury Shirokov; pp. 8, 10: NSP Images; p. 12: Lee Snyder; p. 14: Antonio Diaz; p.18: Afhunta; p. 20: Candybox Images; p.22: Kornilov-dream; p. 24: Dmitrijs Dmitrijevs; p. 26: Susanne Neal; p. 28: Darren Pelligrino; p. 30: Scantaur; p. 34: Pete Saloutos; p. 44: Sebastian Czapnik; p. 52: Magomed Magomedagaev; p. 55: Alfred Wekelo; p. 58: Daralyn